Kindred

NavPress®

Published in alliance with Tyndale House Publishers

KINDRED

A Seven-Session Bible Study on

GOD'S VISION FOR MULTIETHNIC UNITY

NavPress
Bold. Loving. Sensible.
NavPress.com

Kindred: A Seven-Session Bible Study on God's Vision for Multiethnic Unity

A NavPress resource published in alliance with Tyndale House Publishers

The Team:
David Zimmerman, Publisher; Elizabeth Schroll, Copyeditor; Lacie Phillips, Production Assistant; Ron C. Kaufmann, Cover Designer; Cathy Miller, Interior Designer; Sarah Ocenasek, Proofreading Coordinator

For information about special discounts for bulk purchases, please contact Tyndale House Publishers at csresponse@tyndale.com, or call 1-855-277-9400.

ISBN 979-8-89802-004-0

Printed in the United States of America

31 30 29 28 27 26 25
7 6 5 4 3 2 1

Contents

Introduction

Imago Dei. The image of God. The bond that links all human beings together is this: We are each created in the image of God. From our most beloved to our most disdained, this is what we have in common with all humanity.

From the perspective of God's Kingdom, this universal human kinship is what Jesus appealed to when he called us to love our neighbors as ourselves (Matthew 22:39).

From the world's perspective, human kinship is the stuff genealogies are made of. Kinship sets boundaries around whom we marry and who inherits our stuff. Anthropologists tell us that blood-based kinship is the most foundational aspect of virtually every culture that's ever existed. Blood-based kinship is the basis for hard distinctions between "us" and "them," between insiders and outsiders, reaching all the way from family and national ties to clashes across ethnicities.

Jesus turned the world's blood-based kinship constructs upside down. When told that his mother and brothers were outside wanting to see him, he responded, "My mother and my brothers are those who hear the word of God and do it" (Luke 8:21, ESV). In Jesus' Kingdom, kinship is based not on the blood of our ancestors but on the blood he shed for us on the cross. The presence of the Holy Spirit, not DNA, is the mark of our Kingdom kinship, pointing back to that most basic connection we all share—the imago Dei. Our kinship with Christ and the power of the Holy Spirit empower us to love all who bear the image of God and to open our hearts to all whom God calls into Jesus' Kingdom family.

Kindred is a Bible-study resource created by The Navigators in response to the strife-ridden cultural moment we find ourselves in. This guide will help you explore questions of kinship such as these in the light of God's Word:

- Amid such wide human diversity, what is God's heart for humanity?
- In the face of ongoing hostility dividing us from one another, what remedy does God offer?

But these aren't abstract questions. *Kindred* will help you wrestle with Jesus' Kingdom vision for your own discipleship. As you work through this study, ask yourself these questions:

- *How is God at work in my own thinking and feeling about ethnicity and division?*

- *What is God calling me (and us) to as his kindred—lights shining in a world under the shadow of hostility?*

Kindred was created with the following values:

- built on the foundation of substantive personal Bible study exploring God's story
- responsive to the insights of a large, diverse team working in close collaboration
- pointed toward our shared kinship with Christ while representing the stories and experiences of a broad range of backgrounds
- designed for small groups who welcome vulnerability and reject false shame even in the face of uncomfortable conversations
- supportive of honest processing of pain and shame associated with ethnic/racial tensions at the global, national, relational, and personal level
- equipping for discipleship conversations with a strong biblical foundation

Kindred features seven content sessions that explore God's story as it unfolds in Scripture, starting before Creation and continuing into eternity. Each session considers numerous Bible passages, building toward a sweeping biblical theology from Genesis to Revelation.

Expect to spend one to three hours in individual preparation for each session's Bible study. Group discussion should take ninety minutes to two hours. Certain questions in each session are particularly important to personal growth and productive discussion; each one is preceded by the image of a key. Be sure to give these adequate time and consideration.

Some readings reference a particular translation or paraphrase of the Bible. You can read passages in your preferred Bible version, but you can access other versions easily through various websites (for example, BibleGateway.com) or applications (for example, the YouVersion Bible App).

Advance preparation is essential for this Bible study. Attempting to wing it can cause misunderstanding because these discussions touch on highly sensitive issues. So commit to the advance work and come prepared for the group work. The facilitator's guide at the end of the book can help your group move through these discussions circumspectly.

As you work through *Kindred*, you'll probably come across something that makes you uncomfortable, confronts strong opinions you hold, triggers something painful from your history, or irritates you in a way you can't identify. You might also encounter content that seems irrelevant, comes from a source you don't care for or trust, or uses unfamiliar or troubling terms. We encourage you to pray your way through each question, asking God to draw your attention to what he wants you to learn from the challenging content.

This resource was born from two years of collaborative study, research, and prayer. Along the way we have shared our stories with one another, listening until it hurt, wading through mistrust and disagreement. We have shared abundant tears and laughter. It was well worth the labor as kindred for the joy set before us: advancing the Good News of Jesus and his Kingdom into all the nations.

The *Kindred* Core Team
Demitta Clausell-Reese
Connally Gilliam
Judy Gomoll
Patriece Johnson
Dr. Sherry Jones

Additional resources to supplement your group's experience of *Kindred* can be found at navresources.learnupon.com/content-details/3200823/0. A registration is required (at no cost to you) to access the content.

SESSION 1

ONE & MANY

God's Story in Genesis

The story begins as God, the Creator, establishes his beloved image bearers in a garden on planet Earth, giving us the mandate to "be fruitful and multiply" (Genesis 1:28, ESV). We were thriving in relationship with our Creator, one another, and the land around us. But then Satan and sin entered with a vengeance. The result? Doubt and disobedience joined pride and hostility to open grievous divides—between God and his people, between men and women, between siblings and siblings, and eventually between people groups.

But our loving Creator's good purposes for his human family couldn't be thwarted. Even in these first chapters of the Scriptures, we see signs that God would use human divisions and scattering for fruitful multiplication. His plan would involve forming a nation from one chosen man, Abram, and his wife, Sarai. And from them would come many—in fact, a people who would be tasked with being a blessing to all the nations.

Session 1 has seven readings from the book of Genesis for you to interact with. Go through the readings individually ahead of time so you're prepared to discuss them with your group.

Reading One (Genesis 1:11, 21, 25-27, 31)

1. What do you notice about the incredible variety in God's created world?

2. Until verse 26, God has not created anything after his own kind. So he makes us in his image to resemble and represent him. What do you think it means to be an image bearer of our triune God? Whom does this include?

The Hebrew word translated "image" in Genesis 1:26-27 is *tselem*. It's a masculine noun meaning "image," "replica," "pattern," "copy," or "offspring." *Tselem* means that we humans are imprecise copies of God, who is the original! Only humans hold his Spirit and are temples of his glory. This idea is called the imago Dei—the truth is that all people are made in God's image and thus are granted dignity and purpose.

Demuth (Hebrew)—translated "likeness" in Genesis 1:26—is a feminine noun meaning "likeness," "similarity," or "expression." We humans can grow to become like God and share in his attributes. This happens over time as God raises us as his children and teaches us his ways, nature, and character. We become like him—and that brings him glory.

3. How do you see the image and likeness of God in people who don't resemble you?

Reading Two (Genesis 1:28; Acts 17:26-28)

Consider reading Acts 17:26-28 in *The Voice* version of the Bible.

In Genesis 1:28, God gives humanity our first job description—what Nancy Pearcey, in her book *Total Truth*, describes as nothing less than "to develop the *social* world . . . [and] to harness the *natural* world."[1] These instructions are known as the cultural mandate:

> the command to exercise dominion over the earth, subdue it, and develop its latent potential (Gen. 1:26-28; cf. Gen. 2:15). God calls all humans, as those made in his image, to fill the earth with his glory through creating what we commonly call culture.
>
> . . . The cultural mandate is given to all people. . .
>
> . . . to give glory to God.[2]

1. What are some specific ways humanity has fulfilled and is still fulfilling God's command in Genesis 1:28?

2. Acts 17:26-28 is another expression of the cultural mandate. What were God's purposes in making diverse people groups from one man? How would you explain your answer to a child?

3. All cultures, civilizations, and societies are flawed—mixtures of good and bad. Reflect on something in your own culture that has nudged you to search for and find God. What is it? How have other cultures helped you search for and find God?

Reading Three (Genesis 3:1-13)

The serpent enters the scene. It represents Satan, who has rebelled against God and is waging war on earth against God, focusing his efforts on the hearts and minds of humans. The place of blessing becomes the place of curse. Dominion becomes domination.

1. What tactics did Satan use to trick Adam and Eve into disobeying God? How did this impact their view of God and themselves?

2. How do you see Satan's lies and deception still at work today, trying to separate people from God? And from one another, especially across ethnicities? (See John 8:44.)

3. Dishonoring others often takes the form of stereotyping—attributing specific character traits to whole people groups. How do you think stereotypes come into being? What stereotypes do you recall being used during your own upbringing that you now recognize as unfair generalizations?

4. Why is it important to reflect on the role of stereotyping in our childhoods?

Reading Four (Genesis 4:1-16)

Notice how quickly—in only one generation!—Adam and Eve's disobedience bore the bitter fruit of murder. This happened when their son Cain opened the door to anger and sin, stopped seeing himself as his brother Abel's keeper, and killed him. Cain's killing of Abel was the first murder in human history, but it wasn't the last. History is littered with stories of individuals and whole people groups being murdered. Their blood now cries out from the ground in a chorus.

1. What do you imagine Cain was thinking that gave him permission to murder his brother?

2. When God heard the voice of Abel's blood crying out from the ground (verse 10), what do you imagine it was saying? What is the chorus of the murdered singing?

The Mark of Cain and the Curse of Ham

Have you ever heard of the "mark [of] Cain" (Genesis 4:15) being dark skin? For years, many Europeans and Americans abused this Scripture passage to justify viewing Black people as cursed by God and therefore deserving to be enslaved. But the Bible says no such thing. In fact, it says that God marked Cain to protect him, not to curse him: "The LORD put a mark on Cain so that no one who found him would kill him" (verse 15). This passage does not even mention skin color.

Genesis 9:25-27 was also misinterpreted during this same time period to justify enslaving Black Africans. In fact, the "curse of Ham" had nothing whatsoever to do with Africans or skin color. Instead, the focus was on punishing Ham's son, Canaan, which happened when Israel conquered the Canaanites.

What kind of damage can be done if we believe racial lies and the impact of related racist attitudes today?

3. Who else's blood comes to mind as crying out to God from the ground? Think past or present, individual or group, international or in America or within your own family.

4. Why do you think Jesus' blood "speaks a better word" (Hebrews 12:24) than Abel's?

Reading Five (Genesis 11:1-9; Acts 2:5-11)

Languages reflect the beauty and complexity of different cultures. But in the first passage we see the confusion that different languages introduce between different peoples.

1. How do you feel when you are among people speaking a different language or dialect (or even the same language as you but with a different accent)? When has language been a troubling barrier or a helpful bridge to a relationship for you?

2. What do you think God was seeking to prevent or promote by scattering the people and confusing their language? (See also Genesis 10:31-32.)

3. Read Acts 2:5-11. At Pentecost, God didn't introduce a single language for all his people to use. Instead, he enabled people of all ethnic groups to hear the gospel in their own languages. How do you see this passage relating to the events at the tower of Babel, including to the value God places on the diversity of his people?

Reading Six (Genesis 12:1-3; 17:5-6; 18:17-19)

As you read these passages, highlight (or notice) all references to "nation" or "nations." There are five, all of which come from the Hebrew word *goy*, which means "nation," "people," or "Gentiles."[3] This usually refers to the non-Hebrew people (Gentiles) living around and among the Israelites. The New Testament equivalent for *goy* is the Greek word *ethnos* or *ethnē*, from which we get the English word *ethnicity*. Within the last five hundred years, people have come to associate ethnicity with skin color, but this connection was largely absent from the original Greek and Hebrew. When ethnicity is combined with skin color, we often describe it as "race" in modern English.

1. When God called Abram, what did he promise, and what did he command Abram to do? (See Genesis 18:19.)

There are mainly two Hebrew words translated "justice" in the Old Testament:

- *Mishpat* denotes judgment, as in deciding a controversial legal case justly.
- *Tsedeq* (or *tsedaqah*) is a broader term that is often translated either "justice" or "righteousness." It has several shades of meaning, including behaving rightly, speaking honestly and truthfully, deciding a court case correctly, and declaring a verdict about who is in the right.

Mishpat and *tsedeq* often are used together, as here in Genesis 18:19.

2. How might the practices of righteousness and justice be essential to advancing the gospel into the nations and to making disciples?

3. How are you putting Genesis 18:19 into practice in your home and/or ministry?

Reading Seven (Genesis 16:6-16)

There was just one problem with God's promise to bless "all nations on earth" (Genesis 18:18) through Abram's offspring: Abram didn't have any! And his wife, Sarai, was too old to get pregnant. Their solution was to have a baby through a surrogate mother—Sarai's Egyptian servant, Hagar. But Hagar's pregnancy bred trouble, inciting Hagar's contempt and Sarai's fury and harshness. Sarai was so harsh that Hagar ran away. We pick up the story when the angel of the Lord finds Hagar in the desert.

1. When God's angel found Hagar, she was not only pregnant and a foreigner but also rejected, homeless, desperate, and expecting herself and her unborn son to die in the wilderness. What was so personally significant about the name that Hagar gave to God (verse 13)?

2. When victims of hostility and desperation realize that God truly sees, watches over, and dignifies them, how might this impact them?

3. What does God see in you and say about you? How have you been impacted by this?

Wrapping It Up . . .

. . . by personal reflection

1. Which parts of this study resonated with you? Troubled you? Left you hungry for more?

. . . by connecting

2. How does something explored in this session connect with the gospel of Jesus and his Kingdom?

. . . by passing it on

3. Write a simple plan for discipling another person through one Scripture passage from this session.

. . . by noting the key nuggets

4. What do these Scripture passages add to your growing understanding of God's heart for people of all ethnicities and for justice? Here are some ideas to get you started:

   - Every single person bears God's image, giving everyone equal dignity and value in God's eyes.

- Although humanity creates diverse cultures and social systems, they all fall short of God's ideal. So people reach out to God, who alone offers a better culture—Jesus' Kingdom culture.
- Just as Satan deceived Adam and Eve with false ideas about God and about them in the Garden, Satan fuels false narratives about other ethnicities to divide us today.

Below, add some key nuggets (observations and meaningful takeaways for practical applications, lessons, and understanding) that you noticed:

Going Deeper

These first chapters of Genesis remind us that even before God laid out plans for this world, he yearned for a family—beings bearing his image, after his own kind—to relate to him as beloved sons and daughters. The privilege of bearing God's image has endowed every person who has ever lived with innate dignity and worth. But humans have not always lived with this truth in mind. Sin entered the picture, dividing us from God and from one another. The groundwork was laid for interpersonal, national, and cultural hostilities, and eventually for racism.

While humans were dividing themselves from one another, God was laying the groundwork to bless all nations (all the *goyyim*) through his promised redemption. It's worth staying in his story to trace what unfolds next. In session 2, you will continue walking through God's story in Exodus through Deuteronomy.

SESSION 2

THEN & NOW

God's Story in Exodus, Leviticus, Numbers, and Deuteronomy

As God's story unfolds, we find Abraham's descendants encountering drought, migration, and a period of prosperity. Eventually, they become slaves in Egypt. Still, our compassionate God hears the cries of his people and won't be thwarted. He makes a way for them and "a mixed multitude" of others to find their way out of Egypt and into the Promised Land (Exodus 12:38, ESV). This group of Abraham's descendants is his nation, Israel.

With the miraculous rescue of the Israelites as the backdrop, God commands his people to serve him as the one true God and to love their neighbors as themselves. He establishes laws and commands about the treatment of all who are vulnerable: the poor, strangers, slaves, orphans, widows, immigrants, and so on. Still, like all humanity, Israel remains plagued by sin and guilt.

Session 2 has seven readings (primarily from the books attributed to Moses) for you to study. Go through the readings individually ahead of time so you're prepared to discuss them with your group.

Reading One (Genesis 41:53-57; Exodus 1:1-14)

A young Hebrew man named Joseph was sold into slavery by his brothers. The Egyptian official who bought him later threw Joseph into prison on false charges. After some time, he got out and was raised to the level of a prime minister. In that position, he helped his family immigrate to Egypt to escape a devastating famine.*

1. Who came to Egypt during the famine besides the Hebrews? (See Genesis 41:57.)

* When Americans try to conceive of what the word *slavery* means, many of us instinctively imagine the way slavery has been practiced in America. However, not all slavery has looked the same around the world and through the centuries. If you would like to dig deeper, explore the differences between Egyptian, Hebrew, and American forms of slavery.

2. As immigrants in a foreign nation, in what ways did Abraham's great-grandson Joseph and his people both multiply and bless the nations?

3. There came a time when the Egyptians forgot the blessing of Joseph and his people and assumed they were enemies to be feared. What were the Egyptians afraid of? (See Exodus 1:8-10.) How did their fear impact the way they treated the Hebrews?

4. What fears or concerns might be contributing to ethnic and social tensions present today?

Reading Two (Exodus 3:7-10; 12:37-38, 47-50)

After about four hundred years, God responded actively to the oppression of his people.

1. Look at each of these passages and note what God saw, heard, felt, and did. Be specific.

2. Think of a time you cried out to God and knew he saw and heard you, was moved to compassion, and intervened on your behalf. Or think of a time when God did not immediately intervene. Either way, what was that experience like for you?

3. These passages, among many others, were literally cut out of the Bibles that American slaves were allowed to read (known as "slave Bibles"). Why do you think they were cut out of slave Bibles? What are the implications of this misuse of Scripture?

The Hebrew phrase *ereb rab* can be translated "a mixed multitude" or "a motley crew" (Exodus 12:38). This phrase here stresses that many non-Israelites became integrated into the community of faith. The Hebrew word translated "the stranger" in verse 49 (ESV) is *ger*. Both terms suggest that many of these strangers, making up an ethnic mixture of peoples, joined the nation of Israel by putting their faith in Yahweh rather than by being biological descendants of Abraham.

4. Many of us have assumed that God delivered a monoethnic people from Egypt. Look at Exodus 12.

What surprises or touches you about the "mixed multitude" God delivered from Egypt?

Reading Three (Numbers 12:1-9; Deuteronomy 7:1, 3-4; 1 Samuel 16:7)

Moses was married twice, both times to women from other ethnic groups: Zipporah from Midian (an Arab people group) and an unnamed Cushite (Black African) woman. God blessed Moses' marriages but forbade certain other interethnic marriages (Deuteronomy 7:3-4).

1. Why did God restrict interethnic marriage in some cases but not others?

2. Most states in the US criminalized ethnically or racially mixed marriages ("miscegenation") well into the twentieth century. Even though the Supreme Court banned laws against mixed marriages in 1967, many states left those laws on their books for decades. Alabama was the last to repeal its miscegenation

law (in 2000), and even then, only 60 percent of Alabamians supported the repeal. What are your reactions to or observations about this history?

3. Do you know any married couples who come from different ethnic or cultural backgrounds? What struggles might they have faced because of those differences?

4. What blessings might they have enjoyed because of their differences?

Reading Four (Leviticus 19:9-18, 33-34; Deuteronomy 10:17-19)

Consider reading these Scripture passages in the New Living Translation (NLT) and the Christian Standard Bible (CSB).

Much can be revealed about a person or a culture by how they treat both neighbors and foreign nationals who live among them.

1. List below what God expects his people to do—and not do—to their neighbors and foreigners.

DO	**DO *NOT***
leave excess food for the hungry (Leviticus 19:9-10)	oppress or rob them (Leviticus 19:13)
__________	__________
__________	__________
__________	__________
__________	__________

The Hebrew word *ger* can be translated "alien," "stranger," "sojourner," "foreigner," or "immigrant."[1] *Ger* comes from the verb meaning "to sojourn" or "to stay as a temporary resident."

2. Why was it so important to God that Israel never forget that they, too, had once been slaves and foreigners (sojourners)?

3. Recall a time when you were a newcomer, stranger, or foreigner. Were there things people did to welcome, protect, or teach you? How have you done the same for other strangers?

4. Taking into account how much more complicated immigration processes are today than they used to be (with applications, visas, passports, quotas, guarded borders, citizenship regulations, and so on), how is God speaking to you today from these passages about our responsibility toward immigrants?

Reading Five (Deuteronomy 15:11-18)

Consider reading this passage in *The Voice* version of the Bible.

Several different forms of domestic service were practiced in Israel. The Hebrew word *ebed* can be translated "servant," "slave," or "bondservant."[2]

1. Write down some things in this passage that stand out to you.

2. What do you notice from this passage about God's heart for poor, needy people?

3. Pause for a few minutes of prayer. Ask the Holy Spirit to speak to you about your heart for people who are poorer and needier than you are. Ask him about practical ways you already do—or could—love those who are the most vulnerable of your neighbors. Then jot down what comes to mind.

Reading Six (Jeremiah 9:24; 34:8-17)

1. In the law, God declared that every seventh year all Hebrew slaves should be set free. Why do you think this was so important to God that he made a covenant with his people to protect it?

2. Hundreds of years later, when God's people in Jerusalem were under a terrible siege by the Babylonian army, all the leaders and people promised to release their Hebrew slaves. But then they changed their minds (Jeremiah 34:11). God was furious! Why do you think God was so angry at his people?

The American Civil War resulted in slavery being abolished, requiring slaveholders to set their slaves free. But then new ways to keep Black people segregated and in servitude were crafted. This began another bleak period in US history, when some states and cities instituted Jim Crow laws, policies, and social practices that negatively impacted Black people. Jim

Crow laws were meant to ensure that White people maintained power.

3. Do a quick Google search of "Jim Crow laws examples by state." What stands out to you?

Reading Seven (Deuteronomy 5:9-10; Lamentations 5:7, 16; Ezekiel 18:14-20)

Old Testament scholar Dr. Knut Heim is known for having observed to his students that "with very few exceptions, God gets angry about only two things in the Old Testament: idolatry and injustice." The passages in this reading touch on both idolatry (failing to love God) and injustice (failing to love our neighbors).

1. Recent events have caused many of us to reckon afresh with the lingering impact of historic European and North American sins. List two or three examples of the lingering impact of historic sins that you are aware of. Where could you go to learn more about this?

2. According to God's perspective, what are some differences between suffering the consequences of one's own sins and "bear[ing] [the] punishment" for one's ancestors' sins (Lamentations 5:7)?

Individual Sin and Structural Sin

In his article "How Should Christians Understand Structural Sin and Systemic Racism?," Albert Mohler writes,

> The question of heaven and hell is for individuals. It is not for organizations, nations, and societies. But . . . the consequences of sin, the legacy of sin, are passed on to subsequent generations. . . . When you look at God's judgment, it will be meted out at the individual level on the day of judgment, but it is hammered out in history for human organizations, for nations, for civilizations. God's judgment upon those nations shows up in the course of human history, but it is the individuals in those nations who will face the final judgment of God.[3]

3. First John 1:9 assures us that when we confess our sins, "[God] is faithful and just to forgive us our sins and to cleanse us from all unrighteousness" (ESV). How might this assurance free us to join with others in addressing lingering historic wrongs?

Wrapping It Up . . .

. . . by personal reflection

1. Which parts of this study resonated with you? Troubled you? Left you hungry for more?

. . . by connecting

2. How does something explored in this session connect with the gospel of Jesus and his Kingdom?

. . . *by passing it on*

3. Write a simple plan for discipling another person through one Scripture passage from this session.

. . . by noting the key nuggets

4. What do these Scripture passages add to your growing understanding of God's heart for people of all ethnicities and for justice? Here are some ideas to get you started:

   - God uses times of national crisis to force people to reconsider the status quo.

- Prejudice fueled by fear, power, or profit tempts us toward using and marginalizing others.
- God intentionally welcomes and includes "others" into his family. He wants us to spread out and be yeast, not hoard what we have.

Add some key nuggets you noticed below:

To learn more about Black people in the Bible, see the appendix.

SESSION 3

POWER & POVERTY

God's Story in the Psalms and Prophets

God's prophets were raw and real about how God's people were displeasing him. The people's unwillingness to love him exclusively, and to love one another, continued to cost the now-split kingdoms of Israel and Judah. Kings, judges, and other officials abused their power and exerted privileges without considering the needs of poor and marginalized people (regardless of what had landed them in poverty). Painful disruption swept in—from massive geopolitical shifts to deeply personal rifts. But as had been the pattern, God's love wouldn't be stopped; he wouldn't leave his people where they were. His prophets were messengers of the God who offers hope for change in the short term and a promised vision for the long term. Here we read some of the most uncomfortable verses in the Bible. But as we lean in, we see glimpses of God's relentless and passionate commitment to form a people who love him and one another in perfect shalom.

Session 3 has eight readings from the Psalms and Prophets for you to meditate on. Go through these individually ahead of time so you're prepared to discuss them with your group.

Reading One (Amos 5:1, 7-15)

Consider reading this passage in *The Voice* version of the Bible.

During the eighth century BC, Amos preached to the northern kingdom of Israel at a time of relative peace and prosperity. But God's people were also neglecting his laws—offering a show of worship while shrugging at injustice.

1. Through Amos, God charged his people—especially those in power—with many offenses. Highlight or notice the offenses that God detested. What, if anything, particularly stands out to you?

2. What leaders and officials do with their power often filters down to those who serve under them; corruption at the top invites corruption lower down. What illustration of this happening comes to mind for you?

3. Some of us have tasted the bitterness of injustice or the deprivation of poverty—and the shame that can come with it. If that's you, how do you see how God was at work in your life during that time?

4. Some of us have neglected the poor or even participated in injustice out of indifference, fear, a sense of superiority, or something else. If that's you, ask God to speak to your heart about this passage, writing down any message you think he has for you.

Reading Two (Psalm 109:1-8, 11, 14-16, 21-22, 30-31)

Psalm 109 is one of a dozen or more imprecatory psalms in the Bible. These are a type of lament—a way of expressing the individual or corporate cries of God's people. Laments gave voice to Israel's tears in the face of suffering, injustice, or extreme danger. To our modern ears, imprecatory psalms shock us like a desperate scream or curse, but they are not demands for getting personal revenge against one's enemies. Rather, they are anguished pleas for God's justice to prevail.

1. Highlight, underline, or copy down some of the sufferings or injustices that were heaped on David.

2. It is valuable for our pain to be both expressed by us and heard by others. What is the value to you when others hear you cry out in distress and anger? What is the value to those who hear you?

3. Jesus taught us to love our enemies and pray for those who persecute us (Matthew 5:44). Has there been a time when you've done that? What was that like, and what happened as a result?

Reading Three (Isaiah 58)

While Amos was rebuking the powers that be in the northern kingdom of Israel, God sent Isaiah to exhort his people in the southern kingdom of Judah. In Isaiah 58, God points out why he was so angry with his beloved people.

1. Use different colors to highlight the passage in the following ways:
    - **color #1:** the sins of unrighteousness or injustice for which God rebukes his people
    - **color #2:** what real fasting and Sabbath keeping is supposed to look like
    - **color #3:** the soaring blessings God promises to those whose practices align with his heart for the poor and oppressed—his heart for justice

2. When you review this passage, what stands out to you about what God values?

3. Pause to ask God, *Lord, what are you saying to me through these words?* Take time to reflect on his response. Write it down in the space provided.

Reading Four (Jeremiah 22:2-3, 13, 17; Habakkuk 1:2-4)

1. God's prophets repeatedly called out wealthy and powerful individuals for cheating others economically, legally, and in other ways. Have you ever noticed that happening today or experienced it yourself? Explain.

2. When have your circumstances or the suffering of others compelled you to cry out, *God, how long?* Describe that.

3. Why do you think God would sometimes compel us to look at evil and injustice?

Reading Five (Psalm 82:2-4; Isaiah 10:1-3)

God's prophets also repeatedly called out the judicial, legal, and government systems in ancient Israel for being rigged to favor the powerful and greedy over the oppressed and vulnerable. Today we call this systemic injustice.

1. These passages rebuke the nation of Israel for making "unjust laws," issuing "oppressive decrees," and "withhold[ing] justice from the oppressed" (Isaiah 10:1-2). Do you think that still happens today? If so, give one or two examples.

2. Have you or someone you know ever suffered from unjust laws or policies? If so, explain.

3. Where do you fit into God's call to look out for the poor, both individually and corporately? Pause to pray over the following three options and then respond to one of them in the space below.

    - Where local government and charities fall short, what practical step could you take?
    - How might you grow past relying on the government for your basic needs?
    - Learn a bit about where injustice occurs in a local or national social system (for example, education, justice, banking, real estate, foster care, or voting). How might God be nudging you to engage?

Reading Six (Isaiah 9:7; 42:1-4)

The prophets' laments have been echoed at different times throughout the Old Testament and throughout the ages. God has promised to answer all these cries of *When?* and *How long?* The answer started to unfold with the first coming of the Messiah, God's servant bringing the Good News of salvation.

1. When you take a good look at the Messiah, who will set all things right, what about him makes you want to trust him with the cries of your heart and the pain of the world?

We all long for the arrival of God's rule and endless peace, total justice, and perfect righteousness. But we know they haven't arrived yet because the Kingdom cannot fully come without the King.

2. Since we know humans cannot achieve complete peace, justice, or righteousness without the Messiah, what dangers might there be if we try?

3. Even so, from what you know of the Scriptures, in what way(s) does God still call us to seek peace, justice, and righteousness—even if imperfectly?

Reading Seven (Isaiah 54:1-3; 56:1-8)

Israel's covenant-breaking unfaithfulness led them into idolatry, unrighteousness, and injustice and eventually landed them in exile. But no matter how bad things became, God's love never failed. He promised them that his Messiah would one day bear Israel's transgressions and free them to be fruitful and multiply.

1. Why do you think God chose the metaphor of a "barren woman" (Isaiah 54:1) to describe his people at this time?

2. Where were these "children of the desolate woman" (Isaiah 54:1) going to come from? (See also Isaiah 11:10-12.)

3. What might have been shocking to God's original chosen people about the inclusion of "foreigners" (Isaiah 56:3, 6), "eunuchs" (verses 3-4), "exiles," and "still others" (verse 8) in Isaiah's vision of the redemption the Messiah would bring?

4. How would God's primarily Hebrew-culture family need to "enlarge" and "stretch" (Isaiah 54:2) in order to welcome and make room for the additional children God planned to include in his growing family?

5. In this day and age God continues to bring more people, from a vast array of nations and backgrounds, into his family tent—his "house of prayer for all peoples" (Isaiah 56:7, ESV). What changes might still need to happen in our hearts, ministries, and disciplemaking efforts to offer a sense of home and belonging to all peoples, including to those who have felt like outsiders?

Reading Eight (Isaiah 65:17-19; 66:12-16)

The answer to the question *How long, O Lord, before you . . . ?* will culminate at the second coming of the Messiah, when he will set all things right.

1. Highlight whatever you notice about the Lord's final judgment on evil (Isaiah 66:14-16). What do you think about this in light of our desire to see justice done?

2. Now highlight in a different color whatever you notice about God's promises to his servants about the new heavens and new earth he will create. What stirs in you in response?

Quiz on Kinds of Justice

God declares that "righteousness and justice are the foundation of [his] throne" (Psalm 89:14, ESV). Righteousness and justice are meant to go hand in hand. Perhaps the simplest definition of *justice* is "fairness." But in popular conversations today, the word *justice* can mean many different things to different people, depending on the adjective that comes before it. Attempts to achieve fairness for some can create unfairness for others, or they can provide justice through less-than-righteous means. As you have conversations or are asked to participate in justice-seeking activities, pause to discern what kind of justice is the focus.

Try to match these different kinds of justice with the contemporary descriptions below:

1. fair delivery of a fair verdict to the guilty and innocent
2. fair distribution of environmental benefits and burdens
3. fair participation in making decisions or setting policies by those directly affected
4. fair processes and procedures under the law or rules so that nobody is above the law
5. fair punishment that satisfies the desire for revenge
6. fair compensation for a victim's loss
7. fair share in the distribution of economic resources
8. fair reconciliation of offenders with victims and the community at large
9. fair sharing of wealth, opportunities, and privileges in a society

a. procedural justice
b. distributive justice
c. participatory justice
d. criminal justice
e. reparative justice
f. restorative justice
g. retributive justice
h. environmental justice
i. social/economic justice

The Hebrew word *shalom* refers to consummate peace characterized by completeness, soundness, and welfare.[1] Shalom in the presence of God is the ultimate destination of God's diverse family.

3. How much peace do you see in our culture today? In the body of Christ? In your heart? Explain.

Wrapping It Up . . .

. . . by personal reflection

1. Which parts of this study resonated with you? Troubled you? Left you hungry for more?

. . . by connecting

2. How does something explored in this session connect with the gospel of Jesus and his Kingdom?

. . . by passing it on

3. Write a simple plan for discipling another person through one Scripture passage from this session.

. . . by noting the key nuggets

4. What do these Scripture passages add to your growing understanding of God's heart for people of all ethnicities and for justice? Here are some ideas to get you started:

   - In addition to idolatry, God hates injustice and the abuse of power and privilege, especially when it ignores or worsens the burdens faced by people experiencing poverty.

- God's prophets charged God's people with neglecting or even subverting justice and righteousness.
- When faced with prolonged and unrelenting suffering, God's people cry out *When?* and *How long?* in the hope that he will set all things right.
- God promises soaring blessings to people who refuse to be corrupted and actively undo oppression wherever they can.

Add some key nuggets you noticed below:

Answer Key for Quiz on Kinds of Justice

1. d
2. h
3. c
4. a
5. g
6. e
7. b
8. f
9. i

SESSION 4

US & THEM

God's Story in Matthew, Mark, and John

Our story leaps forward with the entrance of Jesus, the God-man who both was before Abraham (John 8:58) and is himself the son of Abraham (Matthew 1:1). The multiethnic lineage of Jesus hints at the work he has come to do—to continue in Abraham's calling to bring the Father's blessing to Jews and Gentiles.

As Jesus makes his way throughout Galilee, Samaria, and Judea, we see him preaching about everything from blessedness to judgment to living water. He heals and honors, challenges and charts the path as the long-awaited Messiah. As he journeys toward the Cross, Jesus consoles and upsets many.

But his commitment to bridge the deadly divides between God and humanity means it is worth it to him to have his innocent blood shed. He follows his Father and calls us to do the same: to follow him into oneness with God and with his emerging, eternal, multiethnic family members—even those from whom we once distanced ourselves.

Session 4 has seven readings from Matthew, Mark, and John for you to meditate on. Go through the readings individually ahead of time so you're prepared to discuss them with your group.

Reading One (Matthew 1:1-7)

Of all the men listed in Jesus' genealogy, it is likely that at least five of them had non-Jewish mothers: Tamar (Canaanite), Rahab (Canaanite), Ruth (Moabite), Bathsheba (Uriah's wife; Gilonite), and Naamah (Rehoboam's mother; Ammonite). By Jewish standards, then, Jesus' bloodline was not pure.

1. What does the lineage of Jesus tell you about the people God works through to accomplish his will?

2. What social and cultural challenges do cross-ethnic marriages face in our time? What challenges do multiracial children face?

Reading Two (Matthew 5:1-12, 21-26, 43-48)

1. What differences do you observe between what is considered blessed in our time and what Jesus calls blessed in Matthew 5:1-12?

2. Some of the people Jesus called blessed were in the midst of very difficult circumstances with no promise of relief. When you, as a believer, are enduring difficult circumstances, what might help you rejoice?

3. In verses 21-22, Jesus traced the relational breakdown between brothers from simple irritation to hatred and even murder. Write down your observations about this deadly breakdown as described by Jesus.

4. What does Jesus command us to do to interrupt this downward spiral? (See verses 43-48.)

5. There can be a fine line between legitimate anger and dangerous hatred. When it comes to ethnic tensions, what has made you legitimately angry? When have you slipped into dangerous hatred?

Reading Three (Matthew 7:3-5)

Every person is made in the image of God. And yet discrimination exists in every person and every people group. The word *discriminate* can mean "to properly discern or distinguish," but especially when it comes to differences between groups of people, it usually means "to make an unjust or prejudicial distinction." God longs for every sinful expression of discrimination to be removed from our hearts because, like a log in the eye, discrimination distorts our vision of those around us.

1. Jesus implies in Matthew 7:3-5 that there is a speck—if not a log—in everyone's eye. Explain why you agree or disagree.

2. Many people believe that ethnic discrimination is a significant log in the eye of the United States, both historically and today. Do you agree? Why or why not?

3. Which sinful forms of discrimination have you noticed in your own life? What hope do you have for overcoming those forms of sinful discrimination?

4. Are you more hopeful or more skeptical that our society can overcome sinful discrimination? Explain.

Reading Four (Matthew 25:31-46)

1. What do you learn from Matthew 25 about Jesus' identification with people who are overlooked and needy?

2. Jesus invites people into "the kingdom prepared for you since the creation of the world" (verse 34). How does this invitation affect your understanding of this Scripture passage?

3. Read verses 35-36. Consider the people mentioned by Jesus and what they need. What is stirring in your heart as you read these verses and reflect on the resources you have available to you (or don't have available to you)?

4. What next step in relation to vulnerable people do you sense the Lord nudging you toward?

Reading Five (John 4:3-39)

The Samaritans emerged as an ethnically and religiously distinct group while most Israelites were in exile under Assyrian rule. Intermarriage between the Jews who had been left behind in Israel and the occupying Assyrians produced the mixed-race Samaritans. When the Jews returned from captivity in Assyria, they looked down on the "half-breed" Samaritans and on the Jews left behind in Israel who had married Assyrian occupiers and adopted their customs and culture. The returning Jews rejected the help of the Samaritans to help rebuild the Temple in Jerusalem and indeed refused to have *any* dealings with them. Likewise, the Samaritans came to disdain the Jews and their Temple and worshiped on Mount Gerizim instead.

1. Many commentators suggest that the Samaritan woman in John 4 came to draw water at noon, an unconventional time for drawing water, because of a sense of shame. What might she have felt ashamed about?

2. What might Jesus have seen in this woman that his disciples—and perhaps even she herself—couldn't see? What value did Jesus extend to her?

3. Imagine Jesus debriefing this scene with his disciples. List two to three principles you think he may have explained to them. (See also John 10:16.)

4. The disciples had to change their perspectives and plans to align with God's plan to grow his family across ethnic and other lines. Practically, how are you modeling and training those you disciple to look past biases to see and value the "others" around them?

Reading Six (Mark 7:24-30)

The Phoenicians grew out of a Canaanite background, emerging around the coastal cities of Tyre and Sidon (located in modern Lebanon). Seafarers and merchants, they sailed the Mediterranean Sea, establishing colonies and outposts along the northern coast of Africa, extending as far west as Morocco. They worshiped pagan gods, like Baal. Their extreme multiculturalism earned them the ethnic slur of "dogs" or "mongrels."

1. The cultural narrative around the Syrophoenicians would have been a source of shame for the woman in Mark 7:24-30. List some reasons she might have felt shamed in that room.

2. When, if ever, have you struggled with your ethnicity, socioeconomic status, or country of origin?

Jesus appears to address the woman using an ethnic slur. This can seem quite disturbing. But the word he uses for "dog" here is not the typical one used as an ethnic slur (*kuōn*); rather, it is a term referring to a family pet or house dog (*kunarion*).

3. How did Jesus figuratively welcome the woman to his table as part of his family by faith?

Reading Seven (Mark 11:15-18)

In the previous session we read of God's desire that his house would be called "a house of prayer for all peoples" (Isaiah 56:7, ESV). The Temple in Jerusalem had a "Court of the Gentiles," the only place where Gentiles and foreigners (for example, Cornelius in Acts 10 and the Samaritan woman in John 4) or those deemed impure (for example, the Ethiopian eunuch in Acts 8) could come to learn about and worship God. The Temple money changers and animal sellers set up business there.

1. What made Jesus angry enough to drive the money changers and animal sellers out of the Temple? (See Mark 11:17.)

2. Why might the chief priest and teachers of the law have wanted to kill Jesus after hearing him speak in the Temple courts?

3. What does this incident reveal about the heart of God for people of all nations and ethnicities?

Wrapping It Up . . .

. . . by personal reflection

1. Which parts of this study resonated with you? Troubled you? Left you hungry for more?

. . . by connecting

2. How does something explored in this session connect with the gospel of Jesus and his Kingdom?

. . . by passing it on

3. Write a simple plan for discipling another person through one Scripture passage from this session.

. . . by noting the key nuggets

4. What do these Scripture passages add to your growing understanding of God's heart for people of all ethnicities and for justice? Here are some ideas to get you started:

    - To be blessed in a biblical sense is very different from what contemporary people associate with blessing.

- Being reconciled with people in your life is related to our right relationship with God. Praying for the people we're in conflict with is one way we can pursue reconciliation.
- God wants us to love others in practical, difference-making ways as an act of devotion to him.

Add some key nuggets you noticed below:

SESSION 5

FAR & WIDE

God's Story in Luke and Acts

Jesus' story unfolds further in Luke's Gospel and the book of Acts, where we learn about Jesus' followers after his ascension to heaven. Luke emphasizes the power of God's Spirit infusing Jesus' miracles, preaching, and personhood. This same Spirit breaks open new paths for the Good News to travel across the ethnic and social diversity of the Roman Empire. The news of Jesus the Messiah is breathtakingly good, but the journey such news follows is undeniably messy. Jesus has come to rupture and remake how God's people think of themselves. In Christ we begin to understand what it means to be part of God's far larger family—to share in the redeeming blood and (surprisingly inclusive) bloodline of Jesus.

Session 5 has eight readings, most of which were written by Luke, for you to study. Go through the readings individually ahead of time so you're prepared to discuss them with your group.

Reading One (Luke 4:14-21)

1. When Jesus returned to his homeland of Galilee, he proclaimed that "the time of the LORD's favor" had come (verse 19, NLT). According to this passage, who might experience the Lord's favor as good news?

2. Jesus read from Isaiah 61:1-2. Imagine you were there, hearing him read aloud. What might have been *good* about what he was reading to those who heard him? What might have been *news* to them?

3. Based on your experience, what comes to mind when you hear the words *poor*, *captive*, *blind*, and *oppressed*? How do you respond to the fact that Jesus highlights these groups as the recipients of the Good News?

Reading Two (Luke 10:25-37)

For centuries the ethnically and religiously "pure" Jews and the "mixed" Samaritans had treated each other with contempt. Two of Jesus' disciples even wanted to "call fire down from heaven to destroy" the Samaritans (Luke 9:54). Ironically, Jesus used the Samaritans to enlarge his followers' concept of "neighbor" and the biblical mandate to love your neighbor. The story he tells in Luke 10 illustrates that neighborly compassion involves concern for the whole person—especially their suffering.

1. The Jews looked down on the Samaritans. What was the significance of Jesus making the hero and true neighbor in his story a Samaritan man?

2. Which character in this story do you most identify with? Why?

3. All three passersby in the story saw the victim with their eyes. But only one looked with a heart of compassion. What people in our world are commonly passed by without being really seen? Why?

4. When have you been mentored, directly or indirectly, by someone from a culture other than yours? What was that experience like?

Reading Three (Luke 23:32-43)

The Cross is at the very heart of the Good News of Jesus and his Kingdom. In the same moment that Jesus' body was torn on the cross, the curtain in the Temple was torn from top to bottom. That symbolized the barriers between God and people being torn down. Forgiveness was now available for everyone, including those who had mocked Jesus as he was dying for them.

1. Try putting yourself in Jesus' place as he was taunted, scoffed at, stripped, and executed unjustly. What might it have felt like for Jesus to go through that horrific experience?

2. How was Jesus able to extend forgiveness to the people who were mocking him and putting him to death?

3. In what ways might you need to be forgiven for matters related to ethnicity and bias? Whom might you need to forgive? Ask the Spirit to bring to mind anyone with whom you need to pursue reconciliation.

Reading Four (Luke 24:46-49)

1. Luke 24 reveals Jesus' last words to his disciples, often referred to as the great commission. Where did he tell them to go? What did he tell them to do? How were they empowered to accomplish his assignment?

2. What nations (*ethnē*) are represented in your neighborhood and surrounding community? How

about in your circle of friends? If you're not sure, how could you learn more about that?

3. How are you living out your commitment to the great commission in your local context and relational circles? Who is on this disciplemaking adventure with you? How might your efforts bring the gospel "to the ends of the earth" (Acts 13:47)?

Reading Five (Acts 2:1-12, 22-24, 36-41)

You may remember from the tower of Babel story (Genesis 11:1-9) that God scattered the proud people of Babel throughout the world. In this story in Acts, the Holy Spirit empowers the newly redeemed people in Jerusalem to be scattered throughout the world, now carrying the Good News with them.

1. The events in Acts 2 involve a diverse crowd of Jews from around the world. How do you think they might have been impacted by hearing "the wonders of God" (verse 11) declared in their own languages and the promise of salvation offered to their "children and for all who are far off" (verse 39)?

2. Imagine three thousand new believers returning from Jerusalem to "every nation under heaven" (verse 5). How did this event further God's purposes to bless all nations and expand his multiethnic forever family?

3. What strikes you about the supernatural events that unfolded that day? Where have you seen the power

of the Holy Spirit shape events in your life and ministry?

Reading Six (Acts 8:26-40)

In session 3 we saw how Isaiah 56 promises the inclusion of eunuchs and foreigners in God's family. Acts 8 describes an encounter between a bearer of the gospel and a foreign, God-fearing eunuch from Ethiopia.

1. **What stands out to you about this story?**

2. How does knowing that the Ethiopian was a eunuch affect your reading? How does knowing that he was "an important official" (verse 27) affect your understanding of this story?

3. Philip connected the passage the eunuch was reading (see Isaiah 53) to the story of Jesus (Acts 8:35). List several ways that "in his humiliation [Jesus] was deprived of justice" (Acts 8:33).

4. How do Jesus' experiences of injustice open your eyes to the pain of victims of injustice in the past and in our time?

Reading Seven (Acts 17:26-28)

In Acts 17 Paul reminds us that God is the one who created all the nations, deciding where and when they should exist.

1. What new insight do you get from Acts 17:26-28 about God's purposes for encouraging so many different cultures and ethnicities?

2. Notice that Paul quotes a secular Greek poet to point his audience back to God. What, if anything, in your own cultural experience (think of art, music, media, poetry, and so on) has pointed you back to God?

3. How near or far away does God feel to you right now? Explain.

Reading Eight (Acts 10:1-48; Galatians 2:11-16)

In Jesus' day, the city of Caesarea was quite a contrast to Jerusalem, the ancient center of the Jews' national history and faith. Caesarea had been modernized by King Herod to honor the Roman emperor Caesar Augustus. It served as a major seaport, the headquarters of the Roman navy, and the administrative capital for Pontius Pilate. With a population of one hundred thousand (roughly half Jews and half Romans), persecution was endemic; the city's amphitheater soaked up the blood of many Christians and Jews who were fed to the lions.

1. What is your first impression of Cornelius? In what ways is your impression shaped by what you've learned about Caesarea?

2. What truths about Gentiles did the Holy Spirit open Peter's eyes to? (See Acts 10:15, 28, 34-35, 45.)

3. Reflect on people you regularly encounter who are significantly different from you—people who sometimes spark your discomfort. What has the Holy Spirit said to you lately about your discomfort?

Acts 10 shows Peter growing in his understanding of God's heart toward the Gentiles. But his old biases show up again later (Galatians 2), and Paul has to intervene to help Peter (Cephas) repent of hypocrisy (Galatians 2:12-13) and self-righteousness (verses 15-16).

4. What biases toward others have you been exposed to? Consider what you might have heard from family members, social networks, your broader culture, your religious upbringing, your school or work, and news media.

5. Hypocrisy can occur when we're afraid of what others might think of us. How can consciously living out the gospel protect you from slipping into hypocrisy and prejudicial postures?

It was a long and hard transforming process for Peter to recognize and forsake his biases. But the gospel of justification only by grace through faith meant that such a transformation was essential. Like Peter, we can't shed our social and ethnic biases through a onetime event. Neither should we expect to heal quickly from the wounds of bias and discrimination inflicted on us.

6. How have you changed over time in your understanding of the relationship of ethnicity to faith? In the space below, write or draw the story of your transformational journey.

A Quick Exercise in Acknowledging Divisions

Social divisions, even hostilities, run throughout human history, as people have divided from and walled themselves off from one another. Identify several pairs of people groups who have historically developed hostility or division between each other. Make sure to include contemporary instances of division. Write these pairs down on opposite sides of the wall diagram below.

1. What troubles you about this image?

2. What do you think is (or was) standing in the way of reconciliation between these pairs?

3. Take a moment to pray for God's intervention in these divisions.

Wrapping It Up . . .

. . . by personal reflection

1. Which parts of this study resonated with you? Troubled you? Left you hungry for more?

. . . by connecting

2. How does something explored in this session connect with the gospel of Jesus and his Kingdom?

. . . by passing it on

3. Write a simple plan for discipling another person through one Scripture passage from this session.

. . . by noting the key nuggets

4. What do these Scripture passages add to your growing understanding of God's heart for people of all ethnicities and for justice? Here are some ideas to get you started:

    - Jesus often challenges his listeners by referencing outsiders in surprising, favorable ways.
    - Forgiveness is a central theme of Jesus' teaching and ministry, and he preached forgiveness to his disciples even after his resurrection.
    - Diversity was a feature of the early church from the very beginning.

Add some key nuggets you noticed below:

SESSION 6

ME & WE

God's Story in Paul's Epistles

God's vision from the beginning was to build a family of holy sons and daughters who would spend eternity with him and each other in joyful worship. Through this Bible study, we have observed God creating, choosing, expanding, and diversifying those who would belong to him. In the Gospels, we read of his plan to deliver them from sin and Satan through the shedding of Christ's blood on the cross. God adopts us into his family and knits us together by his Holy Spirit, weaving us into his new Kingdom family culture. But we still need to unlearn the social divisions and hostilities we carry with us.

In the Epistles, we learn about God's remedy for ethnic division and its close cousin, racism. We also discover God's fathering strategies to grow us from squabbling toddlers to mature brothers and sisters—all in preparation for that great day of Christ's return.

Session 6 has seven passages of Scripture for you to study, all written by Paul. Go through the readings individually ahead of time so you're prepared to discuss them with your group.

Reading One (Ephesians 2:11-22)

Once Christ reconciled us through his shed blood on the cross, the Father adopted us as his beloved children—spiritual infants added to a vast, diverse family with countless other children all desperately needing divine parenting.

1. What are some of the ways Paul describes the Jews and Gentiles being joined together?

2. Imagine yourself as a first-century Gentile from a pagan background—not Jewish, not a God worshiper. How might becoming a Christian change your perspective

on your identity? How might it change the way you relate to your ethnic background?

3. Paraphrase Ephesians 2:13-17 in your own words. What do we discover about the remedy for ethnic hostility in this passage?

Reading Two (Galatians 3:7-9, 26-29)

Our oneness by faith in Christ is founded on our shared identity as sons and daughters of God the Father.

1. How have you experienced the fatherhood of God? In what ways have you discovered God's people as your faith family?

2. How have you experienced unity and blessing within God's family?

3. We know, for example, that Greeks remain Greeks even after putting their faith in Christ. And yet in Galatians 3:28 we're told that such distinctions make

no difference to our oneness in Christ. How have you integrated your ethnic and cultural history, with all its distinctives, into your identity in Christ?

4. What are the dangers of prioritizing your ethnic or cultural identity, your socioeconomic status, or your gender over your identity in Christ?

Reading Three (2 Corinthians 5:14-21)

In 2 Corinthians 5 Paul marks the dramatic transition taking place when we turn to Christ: "The old has passed away; behold, the new has come" (verse 17, ESV).

1. What is it about the love of Christ that compels us to no longer live for ourselves (verses 14-15)?

2. What do you think it means to "regard no one according to the flesh" (verse 16, ESV)? How is this different from acting as though we "don't see color" in our interethnic relationships?

3. What is the "message of reconciliation" entrusted to us (verse 19)?

4. What have you found challenging as you've tried to share the message of reconciliation as an ambassador for Christ?

Reading Four (Romans 12:9-21)

Paul's letter to the believers in Rome clearly lays out what it means to be reconciled to God. But he also describes what it looks like to love one another well in the family of God.

1. Read Romans 12:9-21 slowly, highlighting and noting Paul's direct challenges to the believers in Rome. How would putting these challenges into practice help each of us experience greater unity with and a sense of inclusion in God's family?

2. Central to healthy family life in God's Kingdom is genuine brotherly love (verses 9-10), which includes empathy and humility (verses 15-16). What helps you extend love and empathy toward people with whom you have almost nothing in common?

3. Why is it so hard to resist the desire for revenge? What does God call us to instead of revenge, according to Paul? (See verses 20-21.) Give some examples of what this harder and higher way looks like in your life.

Reading Five (Philemon 1:8-16)

The gospel has the power to transform strangers into family (kindred) and to free slaves to be brothers.

1. How might the gospel have transformed Paul's perspective on Onesimus from viewing him as Philemon's slave to viewing him as his own son (verse 10) and "very heart" (verse 12)?

2. How do you think the relationship between Onesimus and Philemon might have changed when Onesimus

returned with Paul's letter? What circumstances do you think remained the same?

3. How do you see Paul practicing reconciliation in this exchange? In what ways can you identify with Paul here as you practice reconciliation in your own life?

Reading Six (Philippians 2:1-11)

1. In one of the best-known passages from Paul's letters, we find him addressing matters related to privilege: How do we relate to one another as Christ related to us?

2. Read Philippians 2:1-11 slowly. Underline any attitudes that promote or perpetuate division and hostility. Circle any attitudes that promote relational unity and peace.

3. What privileges did Jesus set aside in order to share his intimate access to the Father with us?

4. Paul challenges believers to "count others more significant than yourselves" and to "look not only to [your] own interests" (verses 3-4, ESV). What do these challenges stir up for you personally?

5. What gets in the way of you maintaining the same mindset we see in Jesus through this passage? What

needs to change in your life for you to live in this mindset more consistently?

Reading Seven (1 Corinthians 12:12-26)

Throughout his letters Paul often compares Christian community to the human body, especially when addressing local contexts. In 1 Corinthians 12:12-26, he addresses the health of Christ's body. This is much more than a matter of giftings and roles; it involves union between Jews and Greeks, free people and enslaved people (verse 13). Worldly divisions over racial, socioeconomic, or cultural differences can cause some to conclude "I do not belong" (verse 15, ESV) even as others conclude "I have no need of you" (verse 21, ESV).

Favoritism is a theme in this passage. Paul warns the Corinthians against favoring people with elevated status in the world. He encourages the church to "giv[e] greater honor" (verse 24) to those who lack it, and this applies historically and culturally.

1. The longing to belong and contribute runs deep in the human heart. What do you learn from Paul here about belonging in God's family? About the value of diversity in God's family?

2. What is lost when some people in God's family believe they don't belong to the body?

3. What is lost when some people in God's family believe they don't need those who are different from them?

4. Think about the people in your community. What might it look like for you to "outdo one another in showing honor" (Romans 12:10, ESV)?

Wrapping It Up . . .

. . . by personal reflection

1. Which parts of this study resonated with you? Troubled you? Left you hungry for more?

. . . by connecting

2. How does something explored in this session connect with the gospel of Jesus and his Kingdom?

. . . by passing it on

3. Write a simple plan for discipling another person through one Scripture passage from this session.

____

____

____

____

____

____

. . . by noting the key nuggets

4. What do these Scripture passages add to your growing understanding of God's heart for people of all ethnicities and for justice? Here are some ideas to get you started:

    - Jesus binds us to one another.
    - We are family to one another because of our faith in God our Father!
    - Because we are family in Christ, our relationship to one another is not defined by differences in social status.
    - Our connection to one another as God's family doesn't diminish our individuality; we celebrate our diversity as God's family.

Add some key nuggets you noticed below:

SESSION 7

NOW & FOREVER

God's Story in James and Revelation

"How much better it would be for the Church," writes biblical scholar J. Daniel Hays in his book *From Every People and Nation: A Biblical Theology of Race*, "if we would but grasp the image of the people of God in Revelation and realize that the Church is made up of people from every nationality and race in the world. When Christians think of the concept 'the people of God' they need to visualize what John described: people of every tribe and every language and every people and every nation, all gathered around the throne, worshipping the Lamb together."[1]

This is your final session in *Kindred*! You will have Scripture passages arranged in six readings to study. Go through the readings individually ahead of time so you're prepared to discuss them with your group.

Reading One (James 1:9-10; 2:1-6)

All around the globe, walls of hostility divide the wealthy, privileged, and powerful from the poor, marginalized, and powerless. Even in the church, favoritism is often shown to people of privilege.

1. Based on what James writes here, what levels the playing field between the poor and the privileged?

2. Reflect on your life. Have your circumstances tended more toward wealth or financial struggle? How has your financial status affected your outlook on life? Your sense of connection to God's people?

3. Where have you seen generational factors at play in people's financial circumstances—the benefit of an inheritance, for example, or the impact of growing up in financial hardship?

4. Prayerfully consider how favoritism based on wealth or position has entered your Christian relationships. What are some ways you have fallen into showing special favor to certain people?

Reading Two (James 1:19-20; 3:15-18)

People can feel uncomfortable with anger, as though it is always wrong for Christians to express it. And yet, as we see frequently throughout the Scriptures, anger is an appropriate, authentic, and righteous response to grievous injustice.

1. What is your typical reaction when you see people expressing anger over an injustice? Why do you think you respond the way you do?

2. What, according to James 1:19-20, is the vulnerability of human anger? How might anger get in the way of the pursuit of God's righteousness? On the other hand, how might anger promote the pursuit of God's righteousness?

3. Followers of Jesus are called to distinguish worldly wisdom from heavenly wisdom. According to James

3:15-18, how can we tell the difference between the two? Write down the distinctions you find here.

WORLDLY WISDOM	HEAVENLY WISDOM

4. What helps you apply heavenly wisdom, rather than worldly wisdom, as you respond to injustice in your life and in the world?

Reading Three (James 4:6-12)

Sincere believers will sometimes disagree about how to accomplish God's will in their context. The challenge is to process the disagreement together without slipping into worldly ways of seeing and dealing with one another.

1. What are some ways your pride can slip into disagreements with brothers and sisters in Christ?

2. How might fear get in the way of your shared pursuit of God's purposes?

3. Reflect on a conflict you've had with a fellow believer over matters of conviction. When were you tempted to treat that person with disdain or contempt? What did you do with that temptation?

4. Take some time to prayerfully consider what needs to change in your heart to prioritize unity in God's family during times of conflict. Write down here what you think God wants you to do.

Reading Four (Revelation 14:6-7, 12; 21:1-5)

1. Of all the glorious things God revealed to John in these passages, which ones touch you the most?

2. How might God's promise that the old order of things will pass away (Revelation 21:4) encourage believers from every tribe and nation to endure in the face of suffering?

Reading Five (Revelation 5:9-10; 7:9-10)

1. In Genesis 10, Noah's descendants scattered according to their (1) tribes, (2) languages, (3) peoples, and (4) nations (verses 4, 20, 31). Note where that same fourfold formula shows up in today's reading.

2. In these passages, two things are clear: (1) There is only one human race and (2) the body of Christ is made up of people of all ethnicities, cultures, and colors. From everything God has shown you throughout the *Kindred* study, what are some implications for

   a. your relationships with fellow believers?

   b. your ministry?

c. the way you disciple people?

d. the people (or people groups) you struggle with or consider "others"?

e. the way you worship God?

Reading Six (Revelation 21:22-27)

1. Close your eyes and try to visualize the countless multitudes of God's children worshiping around his throne. What are you picturing? How are you responding to this vision?

2. In this passage, we see God's family represented by the leaders of the *ethnē* bringing their glory to Jesus. What is our responsibility to honor all ethnicities in this life, knowing that Jesus will receive honor from all ethnicities in the life to come?

3. What does the scope of this scene—all *ethnē* represented, walking by God's light—reveal about God's glory? How does the certainty of this future hope shape how you go forward today?

Wrapping It Up . . .

. . . by personal reflection

1. Which parts of this study resonated with you? Troubled you? Left you hungry for more?

. . . by connecting

2. How does something explored in this session connect with the gospel of Jesus and his Kingdom?

. . . by passing it on

3. Write a simple plan for discipling another person through one Scripture passage from this session.

. . . by noting the key nuggets

4. What do these Scripture passages add to your growing understanding of God's heart for people of all ethnicities and for justice? Here are some ideas to get you started:

   - Favoritism has no place in God's family.
   - Humility helps us relate rightly to God and one another.
   - All people flourish with Christ at the center.

Add some key nuggets you noticed below:

This *Kindred* study has explored what the Scriptures show us about ethnicity, justice, and God's heart for the nations. In a time of prayer, ask God to align your will with his. Close this time by praying the Lord's Prayer.

Facilitator's Guide

The conversation that *Kindred* makes possible can be transformational in the lives and communities of participants. But these are sensitive, vulnerable conversations, so good facilitation is critical.

What follow are some points to keep in mind as you move through each session. Review these facilitator aids in advance of your group discussions, and pray for good, fruitful discussion that draws the group closer to one another and deeper into the mission of God that we are each called to.

More generally, here are some priorities to keep in mind for your group to flourish together.

1. *You're a leader, not a teacher.* Fruitful conversation is the agenda of *Kindred.* Focus your energy on getting the best conversation possible out of your group. That means keeping in mind the particular needs and challenges of your people; anticipating, observing, and

addressing relational tensions that could derail discussion; drawing out quieter people and helping more talkative people share space; and more.

2. *The Spirit is moving in—and in between—sessions.* As important as the group discussions are, each group member is also working through this content in the time between sessions. Pray for them, check in with them, and encourage them as they do the homework.

3. *Environment is important.* Give thought to how the meeting space can be made comfortable and conducive to good discussion. Establish some values and ground rules for the group at the outset and share them with the group regularly. Some good ground rules: No talking over each other, no problem solving unless explicitly requested, and no sharing sensitive information outside the group. Pray at the beginning and end of your discussion.

Session 1 | One & Many

Reading Four

The question about Abel's blood speaking is designed to help participants enter this story. Some might struggle to answer it, while others might have deeply considered responses. As the leader, look for opportunities in these responses to steer the conversation organically toward the next questions—about contemporary victims of violence, about the "better word" that Jesus' blood speaks (Hebrews 12:24). For more information on the "curse of Ham," watch the YouTube video "Africa in the Bible: The Myth of a Cursed Race (Part 1) | A Day of Discovery Legacy Series" from Our Daily Bread Ministries (youtube.com/watch?v=RLX92CI5Loo).

Reading Five

Responses to what God was seeking to prevent or promote at Babel might include the following:

- *God was confronting disobedience.* Instead of filling the earth (see Genesis 9:1), the people were trying to stay together in one place (see Genesis 11:4).
- *God was confronting arrogance.* In building the tower, the people were trying to be like God, similar to the sin of Adam and Eve in the Garden (see Genesis 3).
- *God was confronting pride.* In building the tower, the people were trying to make a name for themselves (see Genesis 11:4), putting them in competition with God. Note that God promises to make Abram's name great just one chapter later (see Genesis 12:2).

Session 2 | Then & Now

Readings One and Six

Some participants may struggle to keep in view the differences between slavery as a social system in biblical times and human trafficking or the chattel slavery practiced in the United States (with people being taken from their homes and bought and sold as property). Having some familiarity with the differences may help you move quickly past the distinctions. Read, for example, "The Bible and Slavery" by Andrew Judd (au.thegospelcoalition.org/article/bible-slavery). In any case, enslavement is not God's will for people, so as followers of Jesus, we are to seek justice for those who suffer injustice.

Reading Two

Some participants may be troubled that God waited so long to deliver his people out of slavery in Egypt. They may struggle with the justice of God, given the long delay. Ecclesiastes 3:1-8 reminds us that there is a time for everything. God's purposes will certainly be achieved, but we must trust both his *way* of achieving them and his wise *timing*. Just know that for some people, God's apparent delay may be distressing.

Reading Three

Some participants might not have realized that some biblical marriages were polygamous. Here we're focusing on God's commands regarding marriage across people groups. If participants get distracted by Moses' multiple wives, you might simply say, "Jesus taught that marriage is meant for one man and one woman" and then refocus the group on the question of God's restricting intermarriage with some people groups—recognizing that the false gods of such groups were the problem.

Some participants will be troubled by the fluidity of migration on display in the Bible versus the modern emphasis on national borders. Expect some participants to share from a particular political perspective; expect some defensiveness as well. Notice any tensions people might experience between biblical migration and their ideas about immigrants today. Be gentle with people while keeping the discussion focused on how *God* calls *us* to relate to strangers and sojourners.

Session 3 | Power & Poverty

This session touches on controversial topics. Several readings could be triggering for participants who were or are poor and for those who have been victims of oppression and injustice.

Readings Four and Five

These passages explore how particular systems or institutions have both positive and negative impacts. None of them are perfect; all of them have flaws. Our current political tensions may prompt some participants to characterize a particular system as hopelessly broken or thoroughly corrupt. If this happens, steer the conversation back to God's cultural mandate to rule and bring order to each culture through social and governmental systems and institutions. Help participants remember that the fact that something is imperfect doesn't mean that it's completely corrupt or that we should tear it all down.

Session 4 | Us & Them

Reading One

Cross-ethnic marriage has historically been a point of conflict among some people. This contention is increasingly uncommon but something to be prepared for. As always, pay attention to how people are reacting to questions and to one another during the discussion. Look for ways to redirect discussion away from argument and debate and toward the more foundational question of how we participate in God's multicultural vision for his Kingdom.

Reading Two

Question 5 may be triggering for people who have suffered significant abuse or mistreatment based on their ethnicity. At the same time, the language of the question may be charged for people who are uncomfortable with discussing past harm. Some participants may resist the implicit notion that contemporary people may have derived benefit from or otherwise have responsibility toward the historic suffering of others.

Reading Five

Some contemporary scholars dispute a traditional interpretation of the Samaritan woman's reasons for coming to the well at noon. Some participants may be aware of such scholarship. But in any case, since we can't get inside the mind of the Samaritan woman, it's best to acknowledge that we can only speculate about shame as a motivator here.

Session 5 | Far & Wide

Reading Seven

This reading invites people to think about the cultural expression they grew up with—art, music, holidays, and so on. God has embedded clues to who he is in every culture. That means that every culture has the potential to reveal something important about who God is. Throughout this session, encourage participants to identify and honor God's self-revelation in assorted cultures.

Session 6 | Me & We

In session 6, participants are probing what turns "them" into "us" in God's new Kingdom family culture. Several of these readings challenge us to grapple with viewing God's ethnically diverse sons and daughters as our very own true and eternal brothers and sisters in Christ—our *kindred.*

Reading Three

Among other things, people may experience cynicism and mistrust as they seek to promote reconciliation in the name of Christ.

Reading Five

Paul asks Philemon (an established church leader) to receive Onesimus again, no longer as his slave but as his beloved brother in Christ.

It is likely that one or more of the group participants are experiencing a painful, broken relationship. Invite them to explore what it might feel like and cost them to reconcile where applicable and receive the other person again.

Session 7 | Now & Forever

Conflicts and disagreements in our culture are resulting in alarming divisions and disunity, too often made worse by anger and hostility. The first three readings may expose the pain of division for some participants. Allow them to express their pain without going into detail or naming their opponents. Instead, steer them into the fourth, fifth, and sixth readings, which focus on the coming reality of Jesus' return, when he will establish justice by setting all things right and uniting people of all ethnicities, cultures, and colors on the new earth. Invite participants to consider what it might take to disarm the current hostility and move toward unity in their immediate contexts as preparation for our lives in eternity.

Since this is the last session in *Kindred*, devote the final fifteen minutes of your group meeting to praying in response to all that God has revealed to participants in the course of the study.

Acknowledgments

Kindred was a work of countless people over the course of years. The following people were especially involved in significant ways to make this a trustworthy and life-giving experience. We're grateful for their support and the use of their gifts.

Collaborators

Stowe Campbell
Ken Chi
Serene Chua
Mandy Diaz
Joe Ebuen
Jeff Graf
Delphina Johnson
Dex Johnson
Tom Johnson
Colt Kreeger
Chelonda Marshall
Daniel Medina
David Osborn
Carol Rugg
Anna Snider
Denise Woodson
Felton Woodson
Rick Yorgey

The Core Team

Demitta Clausell-Reese
Connally Gilliam
Judy Gomoll
Patriece Johnson
Dr. Sherry Jones

APPENDIX

Black People in the Bible

A central narrative of the Bible is the story of the people of Israel—the children of Abraham, the people liberated under Moses, the people gathered under the kingship of David, and the people among whom Jesus was born. But the wider world is represented in the Scriptures as well, demonstrating that God's concern has always been for the whole world, not just his chosen people. The following information helps us see how Africa and its people have intersected with the story of God's people.

- *Cush* and *Cushites* are considered by many scholars to refer to Africa and Africans respectively. References to Cush appear fifty-six times in the Scriptures.

- Dark-skinned or Black ethnic people in the Bible are identified with one of these nationalities: Cushites, Ethiopians, Libyans, or Nubians.

- Here are some Black people or Africans mentioned in the Bible:
    - *the Ethiopian eunuch*—the first new believer to be mentioned after Pentecost
    - *Ebed-Melek*—the man who saved Jeremiah's life when everyone else abandoned him
    - *a Cushite woman*—Moses' wife
    - *Phinehas*—Moses' great-nephew, a prominent priest after the Exodus
    - *Simeon called Niger*—an African prophet and/or teacher in the church at Antioch
    - *Zerah*—an African (Cushite) army general
    - *Cushi*—Zephaniah the prophet's father

- None of the Black people or Africans listed above were slaves.

- During the days of chattel slavery, slaveholders attempted to justify their inhumane treatment of dark-skinned image bearers by twisting Scripture concerning Ham, Noah's youngest son. But Ham wasn't Black, and the curse on his son, Canaan, had nothing to do with skin color but rather with Ham's disrespect toward his father (see the box on page 14, "The Mark of Cain and the Curse of Ham").

What insight have you gleaned from reading this information?

Notes

SESSION 1 | ONE & MANY

1. Nancy Pearcey, *Total Truth: Liberating Christianity from Its Cultural Captivity*, study guide ed. (Wheaton, IL: Crossway, 2008), 47.
2. "What Is the Cultural Mandate? Who Is It Given To?," 9Marks, March 10, 2010, https://www.9marks.org/answer/what-cultural-mandate-who-it-given.
3. "Strong's Hebrew—1471. goy," Bible Hub, accessed December 5, 2024, https://biblehub.com/hebrew/1471.htm.

SESSION 2 | THEN & NOW

1. "Strong's Hebrew—1616. ger," Bible Hub, accessed December 5, 2024, https://biblehub.com/hebrew/1616.htm.
2. "Strong's Hebrew—5650. ebed," Bible Hub, accessed December 5, 2024, https://biblehub.com/hebrew/5650.htm.
3. Albert Mohler, "Wednesday, June 24, 2020," *The Briefing*, podcast, MP3 audio, 24:36, https://albertmohler.com/2020/06/24/briefing-6-24-20.

SESSION 3 | POWER & POVERTY

1. For more on this, see Aviezer Ravitzky, "Shalom: Peace in Hebrew," My Jewish Learning, accessed December 5, 2024, https://www.myjewishlearning.com/article/shalom.

SESSION 7 | NOW & FOREVER

1. J. Daniel Hays, *From Every People and Nation: A Biblical Theology of Race*, New Studies in Biblical Theology, vol. 14, ed. D. A. Carson (Downers Grove, IL: InterVarsity Press, 2003), 205.

NavPress

Bold. Loving. Sensible.™

Since 1975, NavPress, a business ministry of The Navigators, has been producing books, ministry resources, and *The Message* Bible to help people to know Christ, make Him known, and help others do the same.®

"God doesn't want us to be shy with his gifts,
but bold and loving and sensible."
2 Timothy 1:7, *The Message*

Learn more about NavPress:

Learn more about The Navigators:

Find NavPress on social media:

TikTok

CP2044